T0099575

Winter Amnesties

CRAB ORCHARD AWARD SERIES IN POETRY

Winter Amnesties

ELTON GLASER

Crab Orchard Review

  Southern Illinois University Press

CARBONDALE AND EDWARDSVILLE

Copyright © 2000 by Elton Glaser

All rights reserved

Printed in the United States of America

03 02 01 00   4 3 2 1

The Crab Orchard Award Series in Poetry is a joint publishing venture
of Southern Illinois University Press and *Crab Orchard Review*. This series has
been made possible by the generous support of the Office of the President of
Southern Illinois University and the Office of the Vice Chancellor for
Academic Affairs and Provost at Southern Illinois University at Carbondale.

Crab Orchard Award Series in Poetry Editor: Jon Tribble
Judge for 1999: Lucia Perillo

Library of Congress Cataloging-in-Publication Data

Glaser, Elton
   Winter amnesties / Elton Glaser.
      p.   cm. — (Crab Orchard award series in poetry)
   I. Title. II. Series
   PS3557.L314W56 2000
   811'.54—dc21
                                                            99-38612
                                                              CIP
   ISBN 0-8093-2305-2 (pbk. : alk. paper)

The paper used in this publication meets the minimum requirements of
American National Standard for Information Sciences—Permanence of Paper
for Printed Library Materials, ANSI Z39.48-1992. ♾

for Elton and Christina

Contents

Three

Acknowledgments

I gratefully acknowledge the following magazines in which many of these poems were first published, some in slightly different versions:

Borderlands—"Bifocal"
Chariton Review—"Cradlesong," "Deathbed Edition"
Cincinnati Poetry Review—"Hymn and Field Holler"
Conduit—"The Effects of Myth at Two below Zero"
English Journal—"Half-Ode at Harvest"
Florida Review—"The Summoning" (part 3 of "Three Poems about Pumps"), "Somniloquy"
Georgia Review—"Eine Kleine Nachtmusik," "Freefall at Evening," "Last Poem of Summer," "Seminary Easter"
Indiana Review—"Spry Declensions"
The Iowa Review—"Sub Rosa"
Laurel Review—"Bird Lady," "First Earth," "Purge"
Louisiana Literature—"King Cake Party," "This Is Your"
Louisville Review—"This Late, This Far"
The Marlboro Review—"Junkyard Blues"
North Dakota Quarterly—"Underfoot," "Forecasts," "The Faith of Forty," "Long in the Tooth"
Oxford Magazine—"Dog Nights"
Pacific Review—"Shadows by Giacometti"
Palmetto Review—"Zero Summer"
Parnassus—"Introibo at 5 A.M."
Pittsburgh Quarterly—"Crows in a Locust Tree"
The Plum Review—"Turning with the Animals"
Poetry—"Dancing Lessons," "Winter Inset"
Poetry Northwest—"Le Piano Introspectif," "Sunny Side Up"
Shenandoah—"Smoking." This poem was reprinted in *The Best American Poetry 1997*.
Southern Humanities Review—"American Flyer," "Nothing of Ourselves," "Principles of Conversion," "Refusing October"
Southern Poetry Review—"Clearing the Ground," "Hibernation," "Epiphany Stick"

Widener Review—"Suppertime"
Yankee—"Seapiece"

I also want to thank the University of Akron and the Ohio Arts Council for granting me fellowships that made possible the completion of my work. And for giving me advice that helped earlier versions of this book take shape, I am indebted to Bob Pope, the late Raeburn Miller, and my wife, Helen.

One

For a long time, I have thought of adding other sections
to the NOTES and one in particular: It Must Be Human.
—WALLACE STEVENS

Clearing the Ground

Everything cold can teach.
—WILLIAM STAFFORD

First month, month I was born in
Far from this day
That stays stuck at zero,
Quicksilver settled in the glass;
Far from this starspray of frost
And the flakes that come down so slow
They're like a phrase suspended
At the end of arguments, white lies
We all learn to believe in . . .

As I have learned, midway,
To put behind me
The rock salt and early grievances,
And let the sun plunge
Down pinwheel collisions of the snow,
Until the dizzy spokes speed up
The late hours lost in storm,
In point-by-point evasions of the light.

This is the mineral spin of winter,
A world of hard water
Seeking its own level: nothing
Stands in its way. This is where
I will start from, night of no moon,
And the wind with its cold drone
Over snow, dragging the dark behind it,
A pedal point of deprivation
That steadies all the shifting keys.

Hymn and Field Holler

You remember how it was, sucking your milk tooth
for the blood beneath it,
and the hogs broke down in mud, above
the consolations of philosophy,
and the ratheels rankling in the corncrib.

It comes back now, your father snarling
his crazy mule around the fields,
your mother hard-eyed in the family pew—
all those stalemates of marriage
overlapping in your veins, pulling and pressing.

And that late summer comes back, when a spangled banty
taught you to strut, and you saw
the bull stacked up behind a knock-kneed cow and learned
to take yourself in hand, beating
like a twang of anvils, the blacksmith's steady stroke.

Tonight you hear the years' hairspring coil and rattle,
the balance wheels roll back
over the deep wrongs, revelations that end the plot,
as the worm-gears turn to unearth
that child still changing in the deadlock of days.

Suppertime

for Mary Oliver

Mother's on the front porch
Calling me
Back from midsummer in the drowsy dusk—
Those rose hues of wool and moss
And the shadows slouching after everything.

All afternoon I felt
The leaves flick in a light wind,
And by a small pool green with blisters
I scraped the scum back,
Letting the tadpoles push and flow,
Loving the struggle
For the two-way bodies they were born to.

Sometimes every step I take
Leads me farther from myself, until the world,
Like a blacksnake pressed against
The clay of the creek bank,
Slides its slow head up
To warn me
With the sun-drugged razzle of its tongue.

And then I stop—as last night I waited
A long time to watch that possum
Stand up from the dead, looking
Awkward and hungry and half-made,
Swinging its bald tail at the moonlight.

It's late, it's always
Too late—that hour torn between
The woods and the cleared field, marooned
Where the bobwhite hides and sings
To itself its own high name, before
The voices deepen in the dark,
Calling their children home.

Introbo at 5 A.M.

In cassock and surplice shot through
with the sweat of dyslexic Latin,
antisemantic as the hieroglyphs
our heathen sneakers print on the altar step,
we pour the watered wine, we ring

the little dinner bells that summon up
the host of the last supper,
always serving more than
our sleepy pieties can waken to,
thickheaded in the heat,

in the close odor of woodwax and forced flowers.
At least the hour brings no hymns,
no tiptoe sermons poised between
the gospel and the pocketbook: brimstone parables
and bromides that pay the bills.

Working the rail, gold plate cradling each chin,
we look down on the saints and the damned
and the bland scandals:
faithful matrons of the mass, handcuffed in rosaries;
a blackjacket juvenile who lives by

the midnight connivance of knives; businessmen
redeeming a pledge, a god-bribe promised
when their typists missed a month.
And after the final fingerbowl, the *Ite, missa est,*
we snuff the candles that lapped themselves

down to a puddle of light, the thin smoke wincing
from the brass shimmer in the brim,
and haul the gaudy missal
back to the sacristy where cruets drain in the sink.
Defrocked at last, knees nodding

as we cross the locked breadbox of the tabernacle,
we hurry home to a black unconsecrated
cup of coffee, rashers of Gadarene,
and the spilled innocence of egg, taking the edge
off all the famished vanities.

Epiphany Stick

So many years erased between
the premise and the end, who knows
what cowlicked misdemeanors set her off?
All I remember is my mother
blaming me with a broomhandle
behind the knees, the epiphany stick,
until I swept the screen door down, lightfoot
in the gravel, in the dead-end street,
one of the charged as guilty, howling
at the air atremble with
the terrible swift coming of her wand,
whose hard sorcery would beat
true behavior into wrongful boys—
for which I now put down
these lines, keeping them
straight and narrow,
while love still whales away
at the frightened crimes of childhood.

Dancing Lessons

Still brooding on the beat,
the needle scratching through each afternoon,
I remember how I sideswiped
the waltz and the hipsprung rhumbas, circling
like a crab with a clubfoot,
and how the hulking girls I pushed around
reeked of roses and sour milk.

Even now I can feel the way my ankles
sank in those slow shoes
when Miss Fahrenheit—too tall, too tan,
too beautiful to be
anyone's mother—first posed against me
and forced my stammering feet
into the blocked maze of a fox-trot.

By whose law was I pressed
to those ballroom drills, those lessons
in civilized desire, as if
my soles grinding through the grit
must pivot to a point serene
as the look on a dustmaid's face that moment when
the count grunts down behind her?

Outside those heavy hours holding up the dead,
I learned at last
what steps I had to take, moved by menace
and the moans of low women,
as all day the radio shook loose my dreams
and gave my body back to me
in a swagger of snares and dirty saxophones.

The Summoning

June sun in Louisiana
and only the faithful go forth,
the children of light—as my father,
summoned to place his repairing hand
on an old truck warped in the guts,
took me down to a hot shed
where all morning three men had spent
their smoke and sweat, and could not
curse that engine back to life. And while
he linked the loose lines and turned
the black cap this way and that,
I sat with one foot at poise
against the gas pedal, until his clear cry came,
Pump the exhilarator! Pump the exhilarator!
and I set the fire free.
O that day when he raised
the spark and clatter, the hard sudden beating
under the hood, I was his witness, alive
to the new mysteries my father worked.

Seminary Easter

1

What did I pray for that first year?
That my cowlick would lie down
Like Jesus in his grave. That I'd catch
Each clumsy afternoon those balls
Bouncing around me in the outfield.
That my dreams would not come
With legs open and tongues aflame.

Brow bent hard against the front
Panel of the pew, I felt the mortuary
Light below the saints creep up
Their plaster robes, their faces
Sweetened by the empty calm that
Glows deep inside a head
When the brain's been removed.

St. Anthony, bring back my lost
Calling and resolve. Mary,
Blue mother of another son
Who took a turn for the worse
At just this season, smile
On this faulty boy who needs
The warm breath of your indulgence.
St. Jude, patron of the dead duck
And the wild goose chase,
Father of the haystack needle,
Get me out of here.

2

Good Fridays when I served
The ceremonies at my old church,
We laid the crosscut planks
On a table top, his broken

Body scaled down from life-size
To a weight made easier to bear.
All afternoon, the sinners moved up
From the dark tales of their confession
To kiss the painted toes of Christ,
My job to wipe away the spittle
Of pious lips pecking at his feet.
But even that clean cloth in my hand
Could not blot out the blood
Leaking where the nails went in.

Here, in this abbey tucked back
Among the pines and ponds, this school
For junior monks and Jesus wannabes,
Stuck on the swampy bottom of
The Bible-beating South, I put my throat
To the haunted lines of a hymn and watched
As the brothers hung between the balconies
The heavy purples of a pall, a curtain
Closing off the stage beyond
The altar steps, a sullen drama
Posed against those props that
Turned to mystery the world I knew.

3
Back home, at midnight mass,
I would carry the paschal candle
In a blur of sweat and wax
And misremembered Latin, incense
Swinging through the nave. And where
There's smoke, there's holy water,
A wet blessing from the dead march.
With the shine of so much satin
Packed inside the chancel, I couldn't budge
Among the priests and prayers, though after
The fleshing of the bread, the lifted wine,
I poured my voice out

In blazing praise of the light,
Late in the soft airs of Louisiana,
Before that early hour when I put
All my bright eggs in one basket.

That first seminary Easter, that feast
Fixed by the moon, I sat waiting
For the drapes to drop, brought down
By a trumpet's wounded cry. And then
The choir kicked in, a signal for
The lamb to stiff-leg its way
Along the aisle, its neck wrapped
In a leash of red ribbon, a sacrifice
The monks would rack up tomorrow,
Fragrant on their plates, their hands
Busy in the black sleeves slack enough
To pull a rabbit from. The windows open,
I could see outside on the lawn
A nimbus of gnats in the cool wind
Where dogwoods blew and bled their petals
Against the risen greens of spring.

If the tomb's vacant, and the body's
Walking on its own again,
What movie were we in — *King of Kings*
Or *The Mummy's Curse*? I loved that
Holy show as much as Hollywood,
Where the gospels go through rewrite
And Jerusalem's built on the back lot.
The morning unwound around me
Like a reel of small miracles.

And when the aftershocks of organ
Rolled out in slow measure, and the bells
Rocked the brick tower above us,
I promised another year, or three,
To whatever spirit forced me here,

And steered my feet from the echoes
To the picnic grounds, where my family
Took me into the safe and patient
Circle of their embrace, my heart
Still uneasy, still hiding
All the frauds of my silent life.

King Cake Party

Perfect circles, if the baker
wasn't drunk, or an oval

like the toy tracks our trains
raced round, every lap the last,

holding to, then flung from,
the small smooth edge of disaster—

another Epiphany, a feast of
sugar shining from the glaze,

crust in the three colors of carnival,
that gaudy goodbye to the flesh.

Twelve days after the wreckage
of ribbons under the tree, and the tree now

giving up its green, our mothers
called us to this custom, this

Creole game of gifts and bread—
eat and you will find, that lucky one

whose teeth don't crack, not gold
or the resin of aromatic gum,

but a bean or nut or plastic
replica of god, a pink inch of Jesus

sold in the trinket shops, half
a dozen to a dime. Once you've won,

you're next to bring these
kids and kings together: a rich ring

of pastry on the table; and mothers
smiling, knives in hand, cutting us

equal shares of the sweet cake;
and milk, frothing on the mouth,

to ease this story down—
three magi from the east, even

a dark one, wise man in the woodpile,
who trailed their star to a stable, and found

a baby bawling for all of us,
purple-faced in his

manger:
which means, in French, *to eat.*

Somniloquy

In that dream where my son stands
Trapped inside the traffic, the cars polishing
Their snub skulls against his skin, I hear him
Cry out to me safe on the sidewalk,
You never loved me! You'll never love me!

And how can I reach him, both of us remote,
Born giving in to nothing
But temptations of silence? Hand held out,
I step into the street, asking pardon for
These battles in the bloodline, this trespass and caress.

American Flyer

Prone with stiff children, the sleds
jitter downhill like little bone-boxes
on a greased run to hell, if hell at last
had frozen over, impossibilities of the proverb
proven true. I'm hunched among the cold fathers
warming their hands at a barrel of broken slats,
the wood-flames a weak rebuttal to the snow.
Once we all felt that first frightened lift
when we launched ourselves from the summit,
steel blades obedient to the way
we leaned or pushed against the pilot bar,
headlong to the end in a windburnt scream.
Now we take on the slow trek upwards,
knees creaking, backs bent to the strain,
each step a test of the blood's ascension
through the heart, dragging behind us
sleds heavy with children, their gloves
sweeping soft reversals on the slope, their boots
brought fast astern, braking our awkward rise.

Junkyard Blues

My father, who could heave
The hood from an old car
High on his flatbed truck,
Is flat in his bed now, is now
As thin as rain, rain
On a tin roof over the junk
Stored there for more than
Forty years, as if the price
Went up with every ounce of rust—
Starters and wires and wheels
And God knows what, too much
To name or stumble through,
A legacy we'll have hauled off
For scrap, for whatever
The going rate might be today.
Born a Catholic, like all of us,
He'll die one, too, buried from
That little church on the bayou road,
At whose early mass he kneeled
On Sunday morning, before the crowds
And the heat could gather there.
And yet, some papers found
When my last great-uncle
Lay fresh in his grave
Said that we came to this
From the deep dark of Germany,
So many lives ago we can't remember,
A lost tribe of Jews, stuck on another
Exodus from the stupid and
The cruel. And I said:
Well, that explains everything.
That explains it all. And now
My father's nothing more
Than bones and breath, as if

He stared at us from some cold
Camp in Poland where the wind
Reeked of ashes and boiling fat,
A wreck among the wrecks.
O put him in the ground
And get it over with —
What difference does it make
Which God he prayed to,
Or why he's dying here
Before our eyes, each day
Weaker and less himself.
My father's still out there,
Sweating his way through
The cranky maze of an engine
In the summer sun, his hands
Black with grease and red
From honest blood roughed out
In stubborn labor. Where we live,
Everything around us is ruins,
Broken, gutted, and cut apart.
And now there's no one
To put the pieces together again.

Winter Inset

for Christina

The bees are still sleeping and she's bored,
My daughter, seven sharp colors by her side, the pencils
Preened and bitten and fitfully arranged

Like remnants of a mangy rainbow.
Hunched down against her will
At this desk where I make the language pay,

She turns her head from mine, and from her brother
Who is testing every key on the typewriter, looking for
The weak link in the alphabet.

Some holiday from school has trapped them here,
Condemned us all to false labor
And the cold probe of hours closing in.

Now her hand moves in protest across the page,
Working the lines in a flurry
Of sullen loops, scratching the axe-edge diagonals.

"Look," my son points, "it's snowing"; and we stare
Through glass afloat with white wings, as if
A great migration of angels were emptying heaven again.

And then she passes me the sketch: a figure
With eyes scorched blue and a sunsquall of yellow hair,
Its open palms cupped under something crosshatched and rough.

"It's got a name," she says, and blocks in
A ground of green letters holding up the mismatched feet:
Angry Girl with Bird's Nest.

Suddenly, in those flat twists, those signals
Tense against the words that light their way, I see
The plunge and pressure of her art:

My daughter pushing back, repairing the day's damage,
Her small portrait halfway between the fall
And the slow underground devotions of the spring.

Cradlesong

for Bob and Carol Pope, and Alexis

Whatever the colors of your birth
And your first wild look out of heaven,
It's not your place
To cry the household down all day.
Let the big dog bark behind the door.
The world's still coming to be loved.

Whatever name the long years build for you,
A breeze of syllables or black croak in the sun,
It's not your place
To dream away the storms of human weather.
Let the big dog bark behind the door.
The world's still coming to be loved.

Whatever the unspent angers of your age
And the damage done by grief, by pity,
It's not your place
To satisfy the stone's hard hunger.
Let the big dog bark behind the door.
The world's still coming to be loved.

Two

One must somehow find a way of loving the world
without trusting it.
—G.K. CHESTERTON

Crows in a Locust Tree

The bad angels are back, come once more,
And not a moment too soon, to sway these feet
From the clumsy paths of righteousness, where we have
Danced all night before the Lord, putting our faith
In the funky chicken and the pigeonwing.

It's good to hear, deep in this purifying breeze,
The greasy trumpets of their tongues break down
The day's defense against darkness, and good to see
A settling of feathers on every bough, black fruit
Among the white clusters of the locust bloom.

You can stone the leaves to a green flutter,
Or even, like Arabs beating their breakfast from
The olive branches of Gethsemane, take a stick
To the stout trunk. But the birds don't stir—
No pinions lift; no shaken nerve betrays them.

Ornaments of evil on the plague tree,
They hang above us, bringing news from on high—
Let the wicked rejoice in their sins, and the swine
Lie down with rats at the midnight revel.
The dove is dead. The crow is born again.

Turning with the Animals

The pig with its twisted prick,
The goat cropping
A stony slatch of weed between the hills—

I take these beasts,
Beard and bristle, wag and slouch,
For all that sours on the tongue and downer parts.

Those days less ironized, before the lockjaw cool,
I, too, would wallow
In the stews and sties, prodigal against

The easy strictures, rattrap beliefs,
Fattening on a diet from the dump—
Condoms, tin cans, dogmas, rags, and magazines

Whose glazed paper decomposed the poems,
Where even love comes undone, bio-
Degradable, below the bray and snout.

And I came back stinking to
The legends of embrace, the mausoleum pieties.
Dreams, darkness, night, death—

All the starved familiar names
Corrupt what they cannot keep down.
They tell too little or too much:

Moonlight teasing the vague pages,
Or a noon sun counting out
Dirt motes on a desk.

I want to lie down again
With the hog and the he-goat,
Brothers of the mud and scarp,

Who never bear more than
Their own patient weight or, restless,
Bargain for a reach of

Heaven above the evidence—
This colony of odd angels
Grounded by desire and design, a homely

Mucilage of hams and four hooves
Truculent against the starstruck earth, testing
The lower limits of the natural law.

First Earth

Her tongue took him quick as a toad's: *toad,*
A brooding bag of leaps whose name came late to him,
And only after hearing unrelieved for days
Her sullen theories and complaints.

What did she settle to, those afternoons
The beasts sprang easily to his lips, and he spoke
The swagger of broad haunches, backwash of fins,
Those loose broods sweeping through the trees?

And in that hour when the winds back up
And stars withdraw beyond the mind, when he
Would smooth his bed down beside her, asleep
In their bower of bindweed and spiked rose,

What was she dreaming then? And why,
In the slow lusters of the dawn, did she seem
A breathing shadow, a sway of dry slopes
Undivided from the earth? He knew only

How much inside he'd given up to her:
Something halfbent beneath her breasts,
Their centers round and ripe as the fruit
She'd picked for him, polished in her hands—

A world still warm from the making.

Seapiece

Standing, as the nightspray starts,
On the stone shore, the slate shore,
You can too clearly hear
The dark thematic rush of the waves' withdrawal.

It is no sound to cradle you,
No lowtide hush and flux
Snuffling from the sand.

This coming in, this mad drag and drain,
This endless hectoring of rocks
Like hammerbrunts from a prisoner condemned
To life for death,
Breath pouring heavy with each stroke—

Who could, for long, listen
To such exhausted labor, or take ease in
The heave and retreat of water at its work?

Not even the moon can soothe you,
Its white sweep spread down the deeper calm
Not like a bridal train, but as the slow
Shine of snails on a wet walkway.

And with the black surf
Frothing at your feet, and the fog
Rising like a sickroom vapor,
You step back
Inside yourself, and hear your heart
Surge like the searoar in a shell
Picked clean, blood-echoes
Breaking through the ruin, the dry spiral
Where all thinking ends in salt.

This Late, This Far

In the mountains north of Montréal,
at that hour when the shadows
step out from the blind vines and birch,
soft paws in the mud rut,

I saw the fox, dirt-dingy,
rib-thin, almost a dog
except for the sharp face, the tipped tail
swept down behind him,

and the even iris of his eye
that stopped me, not from fear
but frozen as he refused
to turn aside those shoulders

squared round in the road,
or shift that wedgehead
looming from his fur
like an emblem, shine in the shag.

It was his mountain,
Mont Tremblant, but my hands
that shook as the wild light
in his look let down

a bar across my body,
the old gaunt warning
that the gates were closed.
Stockstill, still silent,

we stared until the sun
dropped dead and a wind blowing the leaves
the wrong way brought me
back to myself, carried

his cold odor of desolation
and damp dens
into the new air of evening,
air with an edge to it

this late in the long summer, this far
from the low cities of men.

Shadows by Giacometti

It's one of those November days
unlikely in Ohio, when even the sun
becomes an optimist, and gold leaves
glare back like the mother lode.

Inside, I watch the morning lawn,
as rough shapes spindle from the feet,
shadows by Giacometti — the dark
scissor of the legs, the head
an empty oval, a nodding lump.

Who are these shaggy effigies
that people drag behind them,
freak silhouettes that stretch and heel?

They might be some saint
fed up with fasting but still
proud of her wounds, or some rumwreck
driven by the fidgets, a brute
moving in a bootleg dream.

I twist the blinds down
against the light, the diamonds of dawn
that split us from ourselves,
leaving half of what we are
shaken on the earth, a low revelation
level with the dew, the worms'
warm sheen like the scars of autumn.

Freefall at Evening

Over the blue lawn, the lightning bugs
ignite their small lives, no spell of lanterns

asway in a belfry, no fixed signals
like the glitter of a mistress

who summons you across
the marbled miles of a ballroom

while a windy sarabande plucks at
the cold fur above her hemline,

but a tropic of optics, the fire-points
split from an island dance, a jigsaw jewelry

of dusky women, so naked
your eyes feel seasick at the sight,

at the rattle of rainsticks and dry pods,
all the vents and baubles of percussion.

The eyes rise to them
as to compatriot puzzles

that tease and complicate
the native entanglings of the mind.

They breed from the darkness
a broken light, tatters

of the planet they pass through,
gone back to nothing

as you reach for them, or caught,
a spurt of spangles in the hand.

Nothing of Ourselves

The glass glare of the pond, on a day
All clouds abandon, gives back
Nothing of ourselves. This might have been
The world held up to us
Had Adam not pared the apple, or Eve
Not stood there idly coiling
A red tress round her hand, eager to believe
The split flicker of the serpent's tongue,
Invisible inscriptions on the air,
As though the metaphor became
What it called forth, a garden in which
They walked as gods, not that
Stifling paradise overlapped with lions
That licked their feet, or eagles
Screaming endearments in their ears,
Even the vines too friendly, wanting
To touch them at every turn—all Eden
Tame and tangled, forgetful of its place!
Now the inhuman eye of the pond
Stares us down, a light relayed
From the bright heavens, a blinding blue,
As if these still waters still reflect
An earth perfect under a sun
That evens out the peaks and pits, leaving
A level look on a flat land.

Hibernation

for Elton

The turtle wants to sleep.
Winter has turned out the light
Inside his shell and tucked him in,
Head laid out on his parquet floor.

Kept back by this cracked aquarium
From the loam and leafrot he once foraged through,
He could not store the heavy hibernating fat
Packed deep against the dark and snow.

We need to nudge him till he feeds
And trick this long season into spring—
A gooseneck lamp craned down
Across his tired bony back.

So, gently, under a false sun,
We prod him to the seashell souvenir
In which we've counted out
A dozen freeze-dried inchling worms.

Under lids half-drawn, his eyes, not taken in,
Take in the life that life allows. Then,
Wary, slow as a boulder, he slopes ahead,
Clawed feet scratching at the gravelled mat.

Eine Kleine Nachtmusik

Pitchblende; hornblende. Dark ore of the ear.

The night tunes up to A, antenna
And true tone from which
The high-strung alphabet begins:
Vigil of crickets; a cat's cry clawing through
Dilapidated barracks of the rat;
Sparrows eavesdropping under the overhang;
Suck and blow of pine trees milking the moon.

No monks chanting compline down their cowls
Could shake cathedrals like the creak of these
Windstruck sashes, lash of the latch and pane.
What martyr could keep her peace against
The clock's rack and wheel, the water torture of taps,
Trickle of chamber music in the cold bowl? Old feet
Score the hardwood with their cracked heels;
Drumthumps of the unborn
Beat out the belly's lullaby.

And in the homemade medley of the bed—
A little sputter in the syllables, a little
Jitter in the springs—the loose voices
Rise so high the roof can't
Hold them back; they float as though
A million chimneys unrolled their smoke,
Clouds of white noise ringing in
A new era for the ear—

Until it's all a quench of candles,
A quell of touch, the tongues tied
In a slipknot kiss: torpor of silence
Before the loud aubade, as dawn
Brings the darkness down,
And every bird has its own opinion.

A Little Daymusic

You couldn't call it silence, exactly, not when the wind,
That tricky little Brazilian rhythm through the trees,
Still brings to you these sudden sounds: the cat coughing,
A feather in its throat; the bridal flight of the queen bee;
Heinz, that hound of many parts, pouring out his lovesick sobs
To the bitch next door; pine cones going down in the heat;
And some poet, some poor fool who speaks his piece, saying
The same dumb lines since dawn, stuck deep in the alphabet.

And over everything—the gears screaming to a teen-age fit;
Bellow of ballplayers in the beerbelly league; a lawn mower's drone
Putting to sleep the infant insects at the summer roots—
Over everything, there's this small low hum, all afternoon,
A slow lilt that lets you know life keeps its even beat,
Even if, so late in the long season, it still can't carry a tune.

Late Returns in Eden

It's the serpent's day off, and paradise,
A little dusty in the heat, a little hushed
In the lull of unruly leaves, dulls down,
Calm in the long hours of his absence.

Eve lies loose and smooth under a tree
That Adam, busy fitting a word to every beast,
Has not got round to naming yet—a small tree,
Green in the sun, with knobby, anonymous boughs.

If they knew the fruit, they'd know the tree.
The worms, those wet cousins once removed,
Don't care what it's called—they bore through
From stem to bottom, in a drowsy humdrum of bees.

Why won't he come? All the soft afternoon,
They miss his wit, his hiss and dreamy promises,
The way his body pours itself up the trunk,
Tongue testing the air in curls and lashes.

But no grass wavers, and the garden's grown
Slow and cold. O Lord, send them a sign,
That even in this dark they might see themselves,
And be saved, by the sly light of his eyes.

Bird Lady

Two eyes
Can't take me deep enough
Or climb the green reaches of this world—

Spy still out in the cold,
Bush-league voyeur,
Mistress of the peepshow creep,

I hang from my neck
No albatross but a field glass
(Though I have seen that sailor's bird

Haunt the clamjamfry, the offal
Rising in a ship's wake,
Beak hooked like the Wandering Jew).

Others may enter, like Alice,
The wood where things have no name—
Nature Anonymous, one might say—

But I bring to book
Every wingspan in the barrens, every
Warbler on a bough,

Days and weather and *noms de plume*
Cited on my life list,
My roll call of the wild.

I have no use for
Mobs with binoculars, or search parties
Half-sick in a hired plane;

Unflappable,
I go to ground alone:
When fools take to the air,

Wise women fall
On their bellies, at peace
With the worms and the working dead.

Nor does my mother understand
This solitary pleasure, wanting me
To spoon and spark,

To settle on my own nest.
How can I make her
Feel what drives me back

From those breathmint passions,
Ephemera of the lips and lower zones;
Not even a sweet

Aubade of birds
On a bed-blessed morning can overcome
The eggshell inconstancies of love.

Had she read Theocritus,
All that bleating and piping
Composed among the pasture's deep simplicities,

She might have seen what
Draws me to a hawk
Fanning the cloud's brow, or a mole

Humping the dirt,
Or the middle vision of
Moths and butterflies, brushstrokes on the breeze;

And might have learned
How I can spread full-length
In rain and bramble, dust and stone,

To hear the doo-wop trill
Of a thrush or a mating cry
That sprays away the rival claims.

I have the patience of a snake;
I'm stubborn as a fir tree
Green against the topiary snow.

Pigeons I can put up with,
And the bourgeois happiness of robins,
If they know their place.

But I give myself to
Crows picking through the corn brakes,
Conniption of grasshoppers in a fall field;

To the way that chickadees
Bring back the light
After an ice storm, the wintry sun

Flared out behind the low branches
Bowed down to earth, and each dark peak
Tipped in crystal;

And to geese, our fair-weather friends,
Wetbacks forcing the border,
Burnt copper glint in their skin.

Even sparrows on a fencepost
Can make me pause,
Though I'd prefer just once to see

The horned screamer of the swamp,
An Egyptian stilt of cranes, or a secretary bird
That batters out the quick of rats.

With my thermos of tansy tea, my flask
Of blackberry flip, hat tugged tight
Against a tailing wind,

I walk out on this world
And follow the hot flash of feathers
Where the sky breaks through, a flight

Away from those heads bent over
The business of prose and pangs, short end of a line
That goes on as long as it has to.

Dog Nights

Two hours out of midnight and the neighbor's
Whistling for his mutt, that misbreed
Chained all day to the kitchen door,
Slaver and strain when the squirrels tease by
Or when my bootsteps echo on the terrace stone,
And he leaps, ready to rip the next syllable
From my throat. I can hear him now
Panting up the driveway, hard click of his claws.

Dog, I don't know what the dark
Does to you, but you come home calm, your tongue
Unsnarled and lagging, black secrets still intact.
Is it the sudden absence of an enemy, or time
Snapped loose from its tether; or have you
Worked your wet jaws around something
Small and slow? You're just another
Beast the human voice calls back,
No wolf or poodle in the bloodlines, big-boned
And snag-haired, ugly even in the moonlight.

Sunny Side Up

Unlovable, but not unloved,
the broody hen
cackles like a crone the whole town
tarred and feathered. Her hard eye
pecks away at anyone
who peers through the galvanized
loopholes of the coop or steps lightly
inside the deep dung and dark, where she
settles on a ledge, a crusted nest,
and won't come down for corn,
for grit spread to purify the gizzard.
Nothing stirs her; she's fixed
in an excess of motherhood, brown breast
bristling over the globe. Only a hawk,
or a sliding hand, could hoist
the red flag on her forehead
or crank the cutback shuttling stumps
she claims as wings, an engine
revved in neutral on a nowhere run,
refusing to squawk off
in that awkward knock-kneed gait
that starts from scratch and ends with
a keen wind hackling through the ruff,
crack and spatter in the black pan.
All day she cradles the egg, bears down
as if the warm weight of her body
could save it, shell and sac, birdwit
working to keep her from
the bitter repetitions of the roost.

Sub Rosa

At the end of the book of heaven,
that black hole to which all light
aspires and escapes, a white rose
closes over the Virgin and the Florentine
and other emigrants from earth, odor
so sweet it purges and embalms,
a swoon of virtue in a pure retreat.

At bone level, below the rose, it's
nothing more than more of nothing:
an owl looks down, yellow beacon of its eyes
tracking the little sacs of fur and fear
that pant through a plunge of moonlight
to dim woods, sanctum where some shadow lies,
licking the bloodstink from its claws.

Underfoot

This path, laid out
By the logic of roots, by gravel
Cracked from the grind and purge
Of glaciers plowing south,
Leads me deep into the trees.
And I take these green turns,
Unriddling each direction like
The twisted scribble of an invalid,
Though this road holds
No dispensations for the lame,
Uneven, steep, feeling its way
Sidewise around the snags and gashes.

Days like this, with the sunlight
Clogged in the boughs, the close press
Of leaves reaching in, days when
All impediments postpone
The easy compass of the eye,
My steps stall back to origins,
Downward and inward, the earth
Sliding against my sole. And I feel
In the slip and stir of each stone
A galaxy that holds in brace
The bodies it pulls apart,
Always on the brink
Of ruin and revelation. Wherever
This path unwinds itself, I'm walking
On solid worlds that waver under me.

Half-Ode at Harvest

Brawl of wind in the close rows, in the green
Geometries of corn: crow
Comes in numbers, black work of appetite
Bitten to the quick. And when slow machines
Bring down all lines across the field, you can see him
Swag and trespass in the broken acres,
Stalking the stalks, beak and bent wing
Like blasphemies in Kansas. Crow,
Be my medallion: a hard voice
Raking through the shocks and waste of this world;
An eye that rifles the last light, light enough
To wring gold grain from the ruin.

Three

I think we never become really and genuinely our
entire and honest selves until we are dead—and not then
until we have been dead years and years. People ought to start
dead, and then they would be honest so much earlier.

—MARK TWAIN

This Is Your

Engraved invitation to
The coming-out party of the dead,
In autumn when the moon
Rises over shock and husk,
On a lawn where headstones lean
In the pose of Easter Island.
Wear white:
Suits and gowns and cerements,
As though the air tolled with
Perpetual bells of snow.

They will wait, patient
At the end of the mourning line,
For your slow embrace, the late
Admission of your kiss:
Classmates erasing the wrongs
That prove the rule; professors
Tracing in the chalk dust
A pilgrim's map for the mind;
Lovers who let you
Probe and release
The deep damage of their wounds;
Sleepwalking poets, their faces opaque,
Their tall heels and wingtips
Dipped in ink; mothers
Whose lamenting milk
Still drips down
The damp recesses of your dreams.

If you cannot come, if you fear
What music might wind your feet
In the moss and migrant roots,
What drink will score your throat
Like a sky scratched

By the claw-end of leaves,
What wheels will drive you
Home at dawn, where the dew-blades
Bear up the infancies of light—
Then send, in the tremble
Of your own cold hand,
Regrets only, nothing but regrets.

Zero Summer

for Helen

In the ghost zone, in Ohio,
I wake one morning
To bolls of snow,
As if winter had stripped bare
The spiky hedges and bred them
To cotton. Beyond my breath
Spackling the cold window,
I find my first world
Come back secondhand
From the South, and I live
A moment where that bush
Holds the white
Memory of my childhood
In its bent black arms.
And though I'll still pray
For April to lift this
Exile of ice, my heart
Won't give up
The freak season that took me
Halfway to home, wondering
What warm past will I have
Once the sun
Picks this privet clean.

Bifocal

After forty, who knows
Where to look? My sight slides
This way, that way, always
Some warp and startle
In the gaze: a blur
At the outer edge; astigma
In the middle distance.
Now these glasses, ground
To limit errors in the light,
Split the difference between
The lower vision, the higher view;
But any look that's
Sidelong or on the level
Brings haze and waver, no
Crystal witness to the world.
At this age, what should I
Look forward to? It's all
Wince and dead weight,
The years spinning
On the wheel of chance,
Where choice comes down
To darkness or these
Weak and open eyes.
I can't make my mind
Mend this panic in the lens—
Alien lines of the visible
That sway inside the frame,
In the nerves' gnarl and falter.

Long in the Tooth

What shall we call the leaves this evening
When the sap drains down to the roots
And the wind strops itself
Like a surgeon honed on cocaine,
His knacker's knife nursing the heart?

Little obituaries strung out on the rear page,
Rattling the scandals and the box scores; rhymes
Still pining for the unpronounced sentence,
Their passion both to bridge and interrupt; shames
Fevering the cheeks; the minus signs of subtraction;
Smiles of a million vanished cats, all sly
And long in the tooth; the tease of G-strings
Fronting a shaved nakedness of sky; poultice
Where the wet wounds pulse and shut.

Look at them hang in the star loop,
Dead tired but patient against
Their seven moonlit names, our sleights of tongue,
As if they were too much the gentleman
To notice or complain or pass on
The helpless lesson of the dark: that
We are all haunted, but not by the same ghost.

The Effects of Myth at Two below Zero

That snow spanked on the winter pane, it's like
Sirens slapping their tails against the rock,
A come-on that makes the homesick sailors think
Of women primitive enough to beat their wraps
In a dark stream steaming from the jungle, and sing
About the one who got away, a hornpipe tune
That sticks in the rigging and the stacked decks,
All those ropes and poles and pins, and a gangplank
Going over the side, a little wobbly, but still
How else can we get from here to there, there
Where a half-nude half-fish in her seaweed wave
Sucks on a salty finger to test the wind.
It's screaming out of the north tonight, a whine,
High-pitched, that calls the dogs in before they freeze,
A siege of snow, a white horizon only the blind can see.
Inside, we're all sick, and none of these stories
Can stop the storm—the old stories that keep
Seducing the dead in the worst weather of the invisible.

Le Piano Introspectif

She had come to believe her touch
    the way a faith healer
        will close his lifted eyes and let
            his fingers change the face beneath him.

Those early days, her heart beat stiffly
    through scales that weighed and found her
        wanting, the hammers bearing down
            with the speed of guillotines.

All her heroes could not save her:
    Beethoven storming the walls, Schubert
        like a shy bride seducing the headsman.
            Even Mozart she would refuse, saying

There is power in this music
    to make wives rise from their deathbeds
        and berate their husbands
            for the potential of being happy.

But what keys would sweep her past the bars?
    The white ones, wincing if pressed
        for time? The black ones, slow
            as the acrid poise of smoke?

Now her hands lean over
    the blind brink of music
        and step off, each passage falling
            through the airs that take her in

Like one of their own,
    upsway and downdraft as the moods waver
        and the currents pitch freely and steep,
            end over end without end.

The Faith of Forty

In a robe of claret, in furred feet,
Before the insistence of the sun
Brought back the snow-freaked asphalt
And the scarecrow oak, even before
The natural pieties of jogger and dog-walker,
He would prophesy the day, conjure
What might come as fact, defining the indefinite
In a warm room of the cold house.

It was more to face forward to
Than morning's mud in a cup, a plate
Of pig rind and an egg cracked against
The actuarial hindrance of the heart.
It was more than the old hack
Of the glass half-empty, the glass half-full,
More like empty and full at the same time,
The sadness of Falstaff bellied in a jest,

Or that martyr whose wounds went
Beyond their pain, ecstatic allegories of the blood,
As if St. Sebastian were a message board
In the laundromat, tacked to him
Notices for lost cats, rides to Albuquerque,
Distress of those abandoned by God.
Already the mother-light of dawn
Had turned on him, in the gray window

His head like the bastard get
Of a gorgon raped by a satyr, amazed
That the balance of his thought could
Poise inside that ugly skull.
And yet he felt, however restless,
However shrunken and unstrung, a pleasure,
A satisfaction immense as a mind making
The half-inch decisions of its day.

Smoking

I like the cool and heft of it, dull metal on the palm,
And the click, the hiss, the spark fuming into flame,
Boldface of fire, the rage and sway of it, raw blue at the base
And a slope of gold, a touch to the packed tobacco, the tip
Turned red as a warning light, blown brighter by the breath,
The pull and the pump of it, and the paper's white
Smoothed now to ash as the smoke draws back, drawn down
To the black crust of lungs, tar and poisons in the pink,
And the blood sorting it out, veins tight and the heart slow,
The push and wheeze of it, a sweep of plumes in the air
Like a shako of horses dragging a hearse through the late centennium,
London, at the end of December, in the dark and fog.

Dirge in the Chalumeau Register

There is never a *later*, but for most of my life I have believed in *later*.
   —DONALD HALL

I'm becoming one of the old guys,
Mildew behind the ears, moss
In the webbings where the toes meet,

Every ornery morning spent
In a trance of tobacco, in a book
Cracked open at the knees. When I think,

You can almost see a flurry of muscles
From the neck up, anatomy lesson
In the wrinklings of the mind.

I won't waste my day
Deadheading the roses or adding up
A dollar here, a sawbuck there,

Incest of money
Breeding its idiot children. I won't
Remember that first scream

In the fetal accident of birth,
A blood-echo that left me stunned
Like some tourist from Topeka

In a panic over the Roman motormaze
And fountains with their foreign water
And food that never sounded

Like it looked, or looked
The way it tasted. It's true,
I don't know what prayer is,

Though I have prayed
To the lords of poker, and to women
Who paused a lifetime over that one last button

Before the blouse went south.
In the dark of my own sweat,
I have felt myself

Bedeviled by God
And turned the other cheek, certain
What earth I'll soon inherit.

These specimen nights, when the light
From the channels of a cheap TV
Douses the bedroom in the bubbling

Colors of an aquarium,
I drift on the brain waves, wondering
Where this body will fetch up,

As ashes, or under a lawn
So shaved and raked that even
The least weed won't bewilder it.

And sometimes I see a bone wagon
Float down the street, in business with
The backdraft of fire, the slump of dirt,

Its tires inflated like a black cloud
That carries the corpse upwards
But grounds the soul —

My soul, embalmed in ink, and listening
To that murmur the worms make
In their loose translation from the grave.

Spry Declensions

She was always one to take up
last things first, sorbets before
the Buffalo wings and the wedding soup.

And the hats! Some days she would wander in
like an alien life-force, expelled from the planet Xerk
for conduct unbecoming a cranium.

And though her hands pumped like greased pistons
on the spinet keys, firing a song
from zero to sixty with the pedal down,

her words were hit and run, a warble
of wobbly syllables, twelve bent bars
that began *Home, home and deranged.*

Surprising, then, how the poems piled up,
shoeboxes topped with tankas, mislaid pantoumes,
sonnets on Ping-Pong, odes to oatmeal and disgrace—

bard of the pressed posy and the barefaced rhyme!
And there were other wonders that
buttoned her against the cold stare of the crowd:

she could knock down a slug of hardjack
with no tremor in the cup; she was partial to
the hick blue swoons of Patsy Cline; her spry stride

would not allow the tall woman's apologetic stoop.
And when her breath came shallow,
the spark suspended, the starch eased out,

hour on blind hour she would sit
behind the avant-gothic sway of the drapes,
yearlong in a limbo of winter, saying

At my time of life, the time of day
no longer matters, it's always
dark and short.

Refusing October

To stand here, among the overblown roses
And the maples' obituary spark,
And not to see in the sunset
Arson or apocalypse, or in the cold coming down
The shortcut anaesthesia of a new season
Drawn in unrelenting lines
Like a razor's definition of a throat,
But to watch the moon, bone-lonely,
Fetched up at the end of the avenue
In a silver frailty of light,
And then let sleep leach out
The weariness, the dirt of another day
Spent propping up
The rot and rainshaken strata of the past—

How fine fall feels
When the body abandons
All fear of the unrequited life,
And the mind finds in the groundswell
Of spent wicks from oak and locust,
Burnt offerings from the burning bush,
More sheen than even autumn
Could kindle and quench, not as if
The leaves had spilled down from
Dead heaven, but as though they'd burst
Upwards in a flood, a pressured
Resurrection of the pure
Through stone and soil and self,
Earth urging every drop to rise
From wellhead to freeflow, and night tapping
The deep artesian springs of dream.

Purge

Snow lawns, snow trees, streets of snow,
And sky blue as a virgin birth,
The air so cold
Every breath has a clean edge, a clear
Equation solved at zero—
I run into the pure
Pour of morning, where the sun
Sharpens the light in ice swept up
Like splinters from the crack of dawn,

A fifty-year-old frowning private man,
Out on the skids
To pound away this poundage, put back
The rooster pluck of youth,
Gloves keeping out
The gall of frost and the wind's gnaw,
Head packed in wool, but no
Mad-slasher ski-mask on the face,
No earphones breaking down
The poise of silence with
Clumsy lamentations on lost love
Or the God-groveling bombast of Bach.

I feel the freeze between
The stoplight leaflets of autumn
Dropping their hint—
Repent! The end is near!—
And the painted cups of crocus, first
Seedy catalogues of spring.

Out here, at twenty or below,
On the soapstone sidewalks of the neighborhood,
In footsweat and browdrench, each joint
Whining like a tight hinge,

I leave behind all
Kinks in the commonweal, stovepipe opinions,
Victims of the car bomb and the whatnot shelf,
And put this brain and bone to
The next step, the body
Schooled in movements that impede
The unnatural ease of ice and innocence.

Principles of Conversion

How did I, a practicing ex-Catholic
Of Sicilian indolence, son
And lover of the sluggish South,

Take on the disciplines of winter,
And, as if born busy, one of the elect,
Turn a puritan attention to

The deeds of words, a strict
Bricklaying of the language, heavy,
Level at the edge, with

Wings and stories rising from
A mortgage paid down in hard installments?
Or have I always housed this yankee haste?

Even now, as a north wind
Addles the air, the earth sown with snow,
A monk's straight talk still steadies me:

Ora et Labora. I pray this work
Stands high against the years,
When all flesh falls back to salt and cinder.

Forecasts

I can't see it coming
in some rainrot jungle, strange
birds thrilling through the trees,
my blood a feast for
green leeches or a poison dart;
or even down the dry maze
of a desert city, intrigues among
the camel droppings, the dark stalls
of brass and chatter and long-kept dates,
a dirk swizzling between my ribs.

More likely it will come
as one last lesson to the class
on healing the split infinitive,
or after I have spent my time
glossing the way a poet breaks
his line at the end of something
unresolved, and lets the meaning
span the white space while
syntax hangs forever halfway there.

Or when it comes, perhaps
I'll still be stretched out
deep in a book, smoke sloping over
the drowsy page, the words
slowed down to silence, nothing
for my breath but a full stop,
a black hole into which
my share of light draws back from
all that shines and shines and shines.

Last Poem of Summer

Front doors in the neighborhood
Still fly at full staff
The flag of the ladybug, the watermelon flag,
As if summer had not
Sucked in its last wormy breath.

Let me put that in French:
It's all over, bud. Zippo. *Detruit.*

The news hasn't reached
Those couples on the sidewalk,
Pushing their fat kids in a stroller,
Or those women
In their running shoes, pushing fifty,
Who must live on a diet of
Cabbage and kitty litter,
Keeping in shape
For the cold approval
Of the mirror or the man.

Shall I compare myself to a summer's day?

Here's how the day begins:
Rosy-fingered dawn
Leaves its prints all over the lawn furniture,
And some birds with a
Skittery cry have started up,
Backstory to the wretched headlines
The morning paper throws at my feet—

Not the sparrows of Aphrodite,
Or the dove, or the lovebirds
We put behind bars, a parody of parrots,
Their naked singing so loud
It makes even the bull-bent libido
Pull in its pointed horns.

And here's how it ends:
Above the smoke from the late mowers,
A barbecue of stars, a moon
Like gin and tonic on the rocks,
And you in your peacock robe,
Wet silk
That ripples on the limbs and then
Drains down behind you.

I could say my love
Stays longer than
The six dynasties of China, rising
As if I'd lunched on
Goat glands and supped on monkey nuts—
But who would believe that?

All right, I'm the
Runt of summer, rotting in the haze,
A mind of mildew and the red
Hinges of the heart
Stuck shut.

It's the tail end of the season,
The light short and the nights impatient with
A traffic of sticky shadows.
The hot rain
Cuts in on the bias, and I can't
Tell it from my own excited sweat.

That wind
Sloppy in the trees
Will soon bring down the weatherglass
To the first pall of frost.

And what flags
Will the streets fly then,
If not white for surrender, or black
For the piracies of fall?

Deathbed Edition

In the spider-stride of my writing,
I put down these lines
That mull and crest and lag, a blurred book
Meant only to be read
By the black light of the mind,

Each poem a pickaxe that chips away
At the tomb, at Palgrave,
Pages too lonely for applause
And the quick limelight
That gleams, then gutters, then goes out.

And though this throat, when young, was blessed
By crossed candles, I want
No gospel-volume bossed in gold, no Latin chatter
And sweet smoke invoking
Mansions for sale in the sunlit suburbs of heaven.

I want no secret contracts, no cult edition
Bound in the skin of virgins
And signed in blood still pasty to the touch,
With silk endpapers
Sewn from parachutes that flared and failed.

Six decades dumb, I wrote like a rich man
Indulging himself, all checks
And no balances, coming no closer
To philosophy than my lust
Misplaced in that Greek's *Posterior Analytics.*

I remember still the reckless necklines,
Clitrings and amulets of horn;
And how I blundered through each ambush
In the bed, always
At the threshold of some strange breast;

And that moonstirred lover with her red lips
Open for business, her eyes
The Luger-blue of a wasp tail,
Hysterically attractive —
She taught me vows and disavowals.

Do these words marry for money
Or for love? Such questions
Will plump the pockets of professors
And keep the schoolboys up,
Looking for left-hand enigmas in the afterbirth.

But my lines play out their gaiety, a game
Like juggling razor blades,
A sharp music that tricks each mystery, that breaks
Into chants and trances,
Tone rows for ocarina, dog, and rocket ship.

In this new world of weather and tame women,
I live down the days,
Hosannas rotting in the fallen hives,
The sun Decembered into darkness.
What should I crave when the seasons stop?

Gardens were my summer parable,
Barrows of cow dung
Heating and feeding the spilled seed,
Until every row
Split back to green, the ground

Giving in to zinnias, inch by inch,
And mule marigolds,
And loose poppies on the nod, too many blooms
To name or stare away!
And the stems still standing when the heads dispelled.

Earthstruck, I neither studied nor understood
The mechanics of the stars,
Their glitz and zillion disciplines
Ebbing and arcing above us,
A sky ruled out like a diagram.

My vision fits the middle distance, not remote
Or mothery near, but matchlight
In a cupped hand at the end of evening's avenue,
The lure and cipher of
A face flaring beyond my reach.

Late whiskey, and I feel taken by
The terrorists inside
The dream, holding my head hostage,
Demanding ransom, a speech
Confessing on all channels my crimes and flaws.

They hurt me like that rabbit in the briar patch:
A platform of thorns for the soul
Where I can hang by my tongue and lecture
About the rope, once more
Inventing the virtues I rise above.

And now the nurse comes knocking with her tray
Of bogus medicine and pills
Striped like passionate flags—something to fool
The old infant into sleep,
The lullabies of chemistry that whisper to the bones.

And when my mouth draws wide, the words
Slide down the sheets—
Beside me a cup of clear water,
A bowl of paintable fruit,
The whole room ready for the next redeeming death.

CRAB ORCHARD AWARD SERIES IN POETRY